BE THE

EILEEN LAMB

THOUGHT CATALOG Books

THOUGHTCATALOG.COM
NEW YORK · LOS ANGELES

**THOUGHT
CATALOG
Books**

Copyright © 2021 Eileen Lamb.
All rights reserved.

Published by Thought Catalog Books, an
imprint of the digital magazine Thought
Catalog, which is owned and operated
by The Thought & Expression Company
LLC, an independent media organization
based in Brooklyn, New York and Los
Angeles, California.

This book was produced by Chris Lavergne
and Noelle Beams with art direction and
design by KJ Parish. Special thanks to
Bianca Sparacino for creative editorial
direction and Isidoros Karamitopoulos for
circulation management.

Visit us online at *thoughtcatalog.com*
and *shopcatalog.com*.

Made in the United States of America.

ISBN 978-1-949759-31-0

INTRODUCTION

When I browse social media, posts that stop me in my tracks are the ones that make me think, "I could have written this myself." These posts provide me with a sense of relief, a glimmer of hope that I'm not alone in my feelings. I usually feel like a Martian until I hear someone share feelings that I thought were foreign to everyone but me.

As humans, we tend to shy away from expressing our feelings. We're afraid that our emotions make us appear weak. We're afraid we'll be misunderstood, or worse, ignored. We're afraid we'll get hurt, so we convince ourselves that the safest route is to bury our emotions deep inside our heart to eliminate the risk of getting hurt or not being acknowledged.

The more we keep our emotions to ourselves, the more that cycle of loneliness continues. We feel alone, and because no one else talks about vulnerable topics, we start believing that something is wrong with us. In turn, we are even less likely to open up. While it's vulnerable to say, "I'm struggling," "I'm scared," or simply, "I love you," it's needed. It's brave.

I'm writing this book for those who feel lonely. I'm breaking the circle and turning it into a horseshoe so people can come in to join me in sharing and celebrating feelings, emotions, and vulnerability. Whether you're dealing with mental health issues, whether you're simply trying to find yourself in this world and fulfill your dreams, or whether you're looking for people who get you, this book is for you. In a series of short texts, I weave through stories about friendship, love, and self-discovery. *I promise you, you are not alone.*

To Bastien…

Love is
worth
the risk

We live in an age where social media dictates how we feel about ourselves. It's difficult to put ourselves out there when people's likes and comments, or lack thereof, define how we feel about ourselves. I've been there. I'd be lying if I told you that I don't sometimes get scared before I hit "publish" on vulnerable posts. It's not just the fear of people reacting negatively, but also the fear of people not reacting at all.

I once read something along the lines of, "you can be the yummiest, juiciest peach in the world, but there will always be someone who doesn't like peaches." And that's it. I think if we're going to be happy with ourselves, we need to accept that not everyone will see us how we hope for them to—not everyone is compatible with everyone else. And that's okay.

If you are proud of what you're doing, of what you're sharing, then that's enough. Be your own biggest fan. Be proud of yourself for being vulnerable, for expressing something different, and for being unique and standing out when the world pushes you to fit in.

At the end of the day, you need to be your own judge— your own validation.

While it feels good to receive praise and acknowledgment from people you love, and internet points from strangers, if you don't feel good about what you bring to the table, then it's merely a victory. The best validation you can get is your own. It's feeling so good about what you bring into the world that people's validation doesn't matter. It doesn't matter.

When you're the girl who overthinks, everything becomes more complex. You analyze every little detail—every text, every glance, every change in demeanor. Like a detective looking for clues where there aren't any, you have a hard time believing there's no hidden meaning behind what you see. A one-word answer means they're mad at you. No answer means they want nothing to do with you anymore. Your mind skips right past the logical explanation that maybe they're having a hard day or that they're busy. No, it's personal.

You spend hours typing and re-typing a two phrase answer, shaking as you hit "send," and re-rereading your message over and over until they finally answer.

You come off as needy, and you wish people understood that your heart, trust, and feelings have been broken before, and you're just trying to protect yourself. You prepare yourself for the worst in a vain attempt to cushion your soul because if you're prepared for the pain, it hurts a little less.

It's hard for you to believe that happiness can happen to you.

You believe the universe has a way of balancing everything, so even when it's all going well, you're scared that it's going to get taken away.

You constantly feel drained from the intensity of your mind that never stops throwing a tornado of thoughts at you.

You wish there was an off button but there's not. You know it makes it harder for people to love you, so you're thankful for the people who stay—those who know you need a little more reassurance than most.

You know you've found the right person when they love you when you are sad. They've seen you at your worst and they don't run away.

They won't even mention that you're telling them the same story for the third time today. They listen every time like it's the first.

They hug you quietly when you can't express the messiness of your mind in coherent thoughts.

They stay.

In a world where people run away at the first sight of struggle, find the one who stays. They're the keeper that keeps your heart safe.

The truth is, letting go is difficult. It doesn't matter how much your head wants to move on if your heart is still right there, stuck in the past, and filled with hope. Letting go doesn't happen overnight. It's not a linear process. There will be days when it doesn't hurt but there will be others when the simple act of listening to your favorite song or seeing their favorite brand of pasta at the store will throw you into a tailspin. And that's okay.

It doesn't mean you're broken or weak. It means you're human. You can't quickly forget someone responsible for some of your happiest memories. Not like that—not in the blink of an eye. It takes time, so be kind to yourself while you navigate the healing journey. They may be no longer in your life like they were, but they'll forever be in your heart.

Be patient with yourself while stuck in the in-between place—the place between here and there. That place between wanting to move on and holding on tighter. Even though right now you can't see it through your tear-filled eyes, you'll get through this. I promise, you will. And on those hard days, remind yourself that when life doesn't give you what you want, it's because there's usually something better coming up next.

Transitional moments in our lives often revolve around rejection. We're all meant to experience it, some of us more often than others. The fear of rejection can send shivers down even the most confident person's spine. I've experienced it both professionally and in relationships, and it always hurts. That is, the rejection itself hurts. However, what does get easier is the way you bounce back from it and how you learn to let it change you in positive ways.

If you've just been rejected, you have to remember that the person who rejected you only rejected one aspect of you. They rejected the shy girl they saw at the bar, the writer who didn't fit their current needs, or the overqualified job candidate. They never got a chance to see all the layers that make you who you are today. They never got to see your depth, what moves you, what makes you smile, what puts tears in your eyes. They never saw past that one facet you presented.

In a world of billions, not everyone is compatible. This one rejection doesn't define you, it doesn't make you any lesser. You're not losing out on anything because it was never meant to work out. Don't chase after the things that aren't for you or you'll close yourself off to the things that'll actually set your heart on fire.

And in the end, you know what's worse than being rejected? Not knowing. Being the person who plays it safe, the person who's still wondering because they never took a chance. So maybe you feel sad right now, or maybe you're ashamed, but you have something special in the palm of your hands. You're brave. You're the one who tries, the one who takes risks. You're the one who looks fear in the eye and gives it a shot anyway. Those who don't get rejected as much as you do may not have hurt as deeply, but they have to live with that dull pain of a lifetime of what-ifs.

Putting yourself out there is one of the hardest things to do in this world because so much value, internal and external, is placed on acceptance and success. But the only real failure is not trying.

If you're feeling sad about being rejected, you've done something that so many wished they had the bravery to do, and you should be proud of yourself. Damn proud.

We've all had that one person—our person. The one we can't get off our mind. Our first thought in the morning and our last before sleep. That one person you can't forget no matter how hard you try—the one you don't want to fall for because it's too complicated but you can't help it.

It's cruel to be in an almost-relationship. A relationship that does exist, but that's more beautiful in your dreams.

A relationship that makes you wonder if it would be easier if you didn't know how much your heart was capable of loving another human because it hurts.

A relationship that pushes you to try everything to fall out of love with them.

You delete their number so you're not tempted to text them.

You get rid of their photos so you don't admire them with a sad smile.

You block them so you can never see how happy they are without you.

To drive it home, you remind yourself of all the ways in which they've hurt you before.

But that's not enough. They're your person. They can do no wrong. Whatever they do, you still love them just as much. They're stuck in your mind like a fly you can't swat away.

They make you happy. They've turned dark days into bright, cherished memories with just a kind smile. Their touch sends jolts right through you and an intimate moment of eye contact warms every part of you.

Yet you can't be together. It's hard to forget about someone who fills you with such contentment. Someone who consistently makes you feel things you've only ever felt in spurts before. Someone who was the architect of the happiest moments of your life. It is so hard.

It may be little comfort right now, but we all fall hard at some point. Sometimes our hearts choose the wrong person but that's okay. In this big world of ours, there are many souls who can make you feel this way. Your person may seem like the only one but they're not. There are people who feel the way you do about *you*. Maybe you've even met them already. Don't be so busy swatting away that fly that you can't see them.

Fall in love with who they are,

not who you
want them to be.

I wish I had learned sooner that people can
still love you even if their love is
different than yours.

People can still love you even if they don't need you like
you need them. They can still love you even if they don't say
it as often as you'd like.

Sometimes you just have to trust.

Love is worth the risk.

To the dreamers of the world.

To those who feel misunderstood because of the depth of their passion. Those who don't know how to stop trying, how to stop hoping for something better. Those who find smiles on their face, daydreaming about what could be.

It's difficult to incessantly hear how logic must prevail, to focus on the real over the world of the possible. I know the frustration of feeling like you're the only person on this earth who believes in you. How lonely it is to be misunderstood by the people you love.

They want the best for you, they say. They want you to walk down pre-worn paths. To stay safe. To hush your instincts. They expect you to find inspiration in those who make their living doing what you too could do, though not a bone in your body wants it. They want you to do it because it makes sense to them and because you can. They don't get it, but I do.

It doesn't matter to you how prestigious it is. It doesn't matter that the path is clear, laid out with signs and lights. It doesn't matter. If that path is not your own, you won't find happiness at the end of it nor along the way.

There is more to life than traditional ways to pay the bills. There's listening to the voice in your head, learning to notice that voice within, and when you can hear it, believing it.

There's no doubt that your stubbornness may hurt those same people who want the best for you. There's no doubt that you'll see difficulty and pain along the way. But when the sun finally sets, it's you, only you, who may take credit for what may come, and carry the blame for what you never did. Your life is the longest, widest choose-your-own-adventure of them all. You are the one who decides what makes you happy, and ultimately how happy you are.

The road there is mostly blind. And often it's a turn left at a sign pointing right that will eventually lead to where you feel the satisfaction that you crave, that you deserve.

Don't stop trying. Don't stop fighting for what you love. You can do it, and you will. Never give up on lonely dreams, because they only need one person to keep them warm.

Those who are able to bury their feelings may not hurt as deeply as you do, but they will also never love

as hard as you do.

It's a shame that we train ourselves to act the opposite of how we actually feel, forcing a smile when every inch of us is hurting.

It's a shame that we enthusiastically answer, "I'm good," when our mind is screaming, "I'm hurting."

It's a shame that we convince ourselves that we don't care when in reality we can't stop thinking about them.

It's a shame that we hide it all when the secrecy of our deep emotions burns inside us.

It's a shame, but either we do it or we expose ourselves to labels that impact our self-esteem—"too much," "too needy," "too emotional."

So we do it. We train ourselves to bury every tender part of ourselves in the deepest parts of our hearts to keep them safe from the possibility of getting hurt.

Dreams are just dreams.

That is, until
they come true.

There is someone out there who will fall in love with the rawest parts of you–they'll fall in love with parts you don't even love. They'll admire your openness and vulnerability, and see the strength behind the scars that made you who you are today.

One day, you'll find that person you wish you had known for years. One day, you'll find them and you'll never have to wonder whether their love for you is real.

When you meet them, believe me, you'll just know. You'll know.

She wants people to stay after they've seen under the mask.

She wants them to love the raw version of herself as much as they like her when she's at her most polished and smiling through it all.

She wants them to stay after they've seen the pain behind her smile.

She wants them to comfort her when she's sad, even if it doesn't make sense to them.

She wants to hear she's not broken, that she's worthy of being loved, even if she feels too deeply.

She needs reassurance that her softness isn't pushing the people she loves away, because it's hard being vulnerable in a world that so often condemns sharing feelings.

She doesn't see it yet but there's hope. There is someone out there made just for her.

Someone who won't miss the hurt in her eyes when she hides it behind a smile.

Someone she'll be able to be herself with without fear of feeling judged.

Someone who will make her feel good about herself when she feels unlovable.

Someone who will know her darkest secrets and still love her with every fiber of their being.

Someone who will listen as she tells them all about the hardships that made her who she is today. And when she expects them to run away, they'll come closer.

She is all of us.

Strength isn't about being able to hold in your tears when you feel sad. Strength isn't about keeping your feelings inside when they're too intense. Strength isn't about pretending that everything is okay when your soul is hurting.

Strength is the opposite.

Strength is allowing yourself to feel whatever it is that you need to feel at the moment. Strength is feeling deep when the world expects you to hide your sensitivity.

Strength is finding the courage to speak up in a world that has been cruel to you. Strength is letting people in, no matter how many times you've been hurt before. Strength is being able to say, "I'm not okay right now. I need you."

It's okay to need someone. It's okay to need a shoulder to cry on, an ear to listen to you, a hand to hold. We all need someone to remind us that we're not invincible—that we are not alone.

The hurt and depth of yet another betrayal don't have to turn you bitter. You don't have to become one of the hard-hearted.

You don't have to become someone who hurts people in an attempt to get even. You don't.

You don't have control over how people treat you, but you do have control over how you react to them.

You, more than anyone, know what it's like to be hurt by the people you trusted the most—to feel like your insides have been torn apart. You, more than anyone, know that no one deserves this.

Don't turn bitter because of them. Don't let them change you. Instead, love a little bit more, for the people who can't. This is how you'll heal from the weight of another betrayal. This is how.

Anxiety has a way of ruining good things that happen to me. Even when I'm happy, it comes creeping up on me like dark overcast clouds on my sunny day. I convince myself that too much happiness is suspicious, and if I'm happy right now, it's because something terrible is going to happen soon. Anxiety is not rational. Anxiety is knowing all about the logic of something impossible happening and still convincing yourself that there is a crack somewhere in that logic and that the 1-in-a-million chance of something bad happening will definitely happen to you.

Anxiety also comes with an intense mind that never stops ruminating, so much so that it becomes a form of torture. I sometimes wake up in the middle of the night sweating, thinking of the things I could have done better, like that one text a few months ago that maybe I should have worded slightly differently.

My anxiety doesn't only affect me, it affects the people around me, too. Anxiety makes my relationships harder.

I can be paranoid, and too sensitive—too much, too me. If I see changes in a friend's behavior, I come up with tons of hypothetical scenarios that would explain why they hate me right now, because if they didn't answer my text yet, clearly they do hate me. I skip right past the logical explanation that they're just busy, or feeling down about something wholly unrelated to me. I convince myself that they're mad, that I screwed up, and that they've finally had enough of my overthinking mind. I live in constant fear of losing the people I love. I care so much that just knowing that there's a possibility that good things could end is unbearable to me.

My anxiety is trying to protect me. It's preparing me for the worst so I have a chance to grab a parachute to soften the fall. One of the downfalls, though, is that to prevent potential heartbreak, I distance myself from the people I love. It ends up affecting the relationship, even though in reality there was nothing to protect myself against to begin with.

My anxiety and I, we've gone through a lot together, and sometimes it's difficult for us to believe that people can stay even when we're not our best selves.

It's difficult for us to believe that there are people that actually stay through storms that life throws at us. It feels like utopia to believe that forever-friends do exist and that they can happen to us too. But forever-friends exist, and for them I'm thankful.

I know my need for reassurance can come across as clingy, and I feel like I constantly have to apologize for it. But I want my friends to know that this isn't something I can control yet. I know better than anyone how incredibly annoying an overactive mind is. I live with it, and, believe me, I wish I'd found the off button already.

Above all, I want my friends to know that having them by my side is the most beautiful gift that a girl like me, a girl with anxiety, could ask for. To the friends who stay, thank you.

When you lose a friend, a little part of you dies. It hurts even more when the end is slow. It starts with them taking a bit longer to answer your texts. At first, you don't think much of it. Well, you do, but you tell yourself that it's your anxiety talking. They're probably just busy and have a lot on their plate. But then it happens again. And again. The daily phone calls? Gone. Not even weekly now.

Months go by and things don't get better. They've become a stranger, that one friend who knew your deepest secrets and whom you trusted and loved. They're gone. Gone from your life, but not from your heart, and that's why it hurts. You didn't want that friendship to end. It wasn't your choice.

Deep down you know people often grow apart. But with this friendship—this person—you thought it was different. You didn't think anything could break that bond between you. Not even time. Especially not time. But it happened. There wasn't a fight, nor a reason, but little by little you felt the distance. It was a slow death.

When you lose the one friend you thought would be in your life forever, you have to grieve. You grieve the beginning of the relationship. You grieve what you used to be. You grieve the tears you cried together, the laughs you had, and the texts that never went unanswered. You miss it.

You may even feel silly for being so sad. After all, you didn't live together, and you were never going to get married or have kids together; it wasn't like that. But none of that matters. You loved them. You still do.

Losing someone you love is a painful process no matter the circumstances.

I know you can't help but wonder why life keeps throwing people at you who aren't meant to stay.

I know you wonder if it's even worth investing in relationships if they're all meant to expire.

I know you wonder if temporary happiness is worth the pain. You wonder if you should walk away before you inevitably suffer. But maybe relationships just aren't meant to last.

Maybe there's beauty in its passing moment. Maybe life puts people in our path simply for the lessons they teach us and how they inspire us to change, to better ourselves, and to not commit the same mistakes again.

You have to believe that this person crossed your path at one point in time because you both needed each other. So hold on to the good memories, even if it hurts. Hold them tight.

Trust

I only write about my struggles. It's true.

I write to scream my pain through these silent words.

I write when my soul burns hot.

When I'm hurt.

When the pressure of it all can only go one of two ways.

For me, it's simpler to put pen on paper than trying to speak, to explain, to converse.

It's pain that presses my fingertips into the keyboard.

I don't write when I'm having a great day.

So if I don't write about you, my love, be easy.

Rest assured.

I hope you find the people who hear "I need your help" behind your bogus "I'm good," the ones who know what lies behind your silence, and the ones who will see the love through your anger. But also the ones who will understand you and forgive you when you've been a pale representation of yourself. The ones who stay when others have left you in the past.

I hope you surround yourself with the right people. Not those who are only here when everything's shiny, but those who stay when you're so overwhelmed that you can't even put your pain into words.

I hope you find the people who make you feel loved when you feel unlovable. The ones who will never make you doubt your self-worth. The ones with whom you can be honest and who will be honest right back to you.

I hope you find the ones who'll break down your walls, yet stay after seeing the scars on your soul. The ones who will give you tough love when you're off the mark. The ones who will reassure you that everything's gonna be okay when all you see is darkness. The ones who will laugh with you until both your faces hurt. And the ones who will hug you instead of judging when you're crying, because on that particular day you can't hold it together anymore.

I hope you find the people who will never make you feel like your love is too much and the people who make you a priority even when it's not convenient.

In a world that can be harsh, I wish for you to find the people who will make you feel like you're not alone. You might feel like an island right now but you are not alone—you just need to find your people.

It's okay to be afraid to lose them, because being
afraid to lose that relationship is a sign
that it's worth fighting for.
So, fight for it.

Fight for the people you love, those who inspire you. Fight
for the relationships that scare you.

Keep fighting.

She hears incessantly that she needs to get her head out of the clouds and back to earth. But she couldn't if she wanted to.

Dreams help her cope with the present, whatever may be ensuing. Dreams are her motivation to keep going when the world tries to beat her down.

There's beauty in believing in dreams, for they can brighten even the dullest day. Believe me, there are no dreams crazy enough that they're not worth chasing after.

I know what goes on in this beautiful mind of yours.

You don't show your pain because you heard that to be vulnerable is to be weak, that crying is a flaw, and that you need to get back up as soon as you fall.

But you don't. I'm here to tell you that it's okay if you can't. It's okay.

The truth is, if someone wants to be in your life, they will be. They will be, whether their day was hectic or not. They will be, no matter who texts whom first. They'll be here when life is beautiful and you laugh together until your guts hurt, but they'll also be here when life is difficult. They'll be here on those lonely nights when you can't fall asleep, and those mornings when you can't get up because your heart weighs too much. They will be there when it's easy and when it's not.

If someone wants to be in your life, you'll never have to doubt it. You'll just know. There won't be any mixed signals. There won't be tears about things between you being so much better yesterday than they are today. There won't be confusion, and you won't have to wonder how your relationship can be a fairytale one day and a drama the next.

Let today be the day you stop lying to yourself. Let it be the day you move on, the day you forgive yourself for loving them too deeply, and for investing time and pieces of your heart in someone who wasn't ready for your love.

Society puts so much emphasis on success that it prevents many of us from going after our dreams—from going after what makes us happy, what sends shivers down our spines and butterflies in our stomachs. The need to succeed is so fundamental in our minds that it's terrifying for many of us to try at all.

I don't let the fear of failure stop me from trying anymore. I take risks. Some may call it crazy because I get hurt more than the average person, but I find it liberating. I don't have to live with that dull, constant pain of not knowing. I don't have to live with the what-ifs.

I dedicate my free time to my wildest dreams, even when I know the chances of success are slim. I don't hesitate to put myself out there, even when I know I'll be made fun of because people are too often expected to hide the intensity of their minds. And I fight for my relationships until there is not an ounce of hope left. I risk my heart, hoping that it will pay off. And if it doesn't, well, if it doesn't, then I know I did my part. There's no remorse. Regrets, maybe, sometimes, but regrets fade away.

Regrets are sharp pain, but temporary if you keep moving. Remorse, on the other hand, slowly eats your soul with the daily self-questioning of what could have been. What would have happened if I'd tried?

When I'm unsure whether to go for something or not, I have to ask myself, "Would I have done it if I wasn't afraid of failure?" 9 times out of 10, the answer is yes.

More times than not, the only thing stopping you from trying is the fear of failure and rejection.

You don't get anything without risk. Believe me, the pain you'll feel if your expectations aren't met is nothing compared to the dark, immutable remorse of the pain from not being brave enough to try. Do not let the fear of failure stop you from trying.

To the people fighting invisible battles, the
people who silently hurt from
the fear that their feelings
are a burden, this is a reminder that you are not alone.

You are worth it.

And I see you.

Sometimes, in relationships, it just doesn't work no matter how hard you try and you're left with the ruins of a relationship that once meant everything to you. It happens slowly. You don't just wake up one day and decide it isn't working anymore. It's a slow drip and with each drop the strength of your relationship weakens.

It starts with futile arguments. At first, you laugh them off until eventually, it's not funny. Until your quirks become an annoyance instead of something that makes them smile. Until the way he looks at you makes you feel insecure instead of confident. Until you always choose work instead of a movie with him. Until he always chooses his friends over dinner with you.

At first, you convince yourself that these feelings are normal, that no relationship is perfect and that you just have to keep trying. You remember the memories of that person who once made you feel whole, and you hang onto them tightly. You let them remind you that it's worth drawing your sword for this.

Oh, you fight at first. You get through the waves together, and after each hit, you get back up. But each battle cools your relationship's spark. Resentment builds until one day the final wave knocks you down and you don't have the force to fight it anymore.

I know that you're wondering why life keeps putting people in your path who aren't meant to stay, but you have to hang on.

I'm proud of the way you gave your heart away and undressed all the layers that protect your soul because that person made you feel safe.

I'm proud of how you gave them your whole, how you didn't protect yourself and opened up to them.

I'm proud of the way you showed your scars and made yourself vulnerable.

I think it's beautiful the way you cared for them, the way you were yourself with them without fear of them walking away.

You wanted a full-time person, but they could only be your once-in-a-while. Listen, people change and feelings change too, and that has nothing to do with you. You didn't screw up—it's life.

I know it doesn't make it any less painful right now when your lungs still breathe their name. I know you're angry at life for showing you happiness so briefly, for giving you what you'd always wanted, and then taking it away from you. It's cruel. I agree.

But you don't have to regret this relationship. There really is a lesson to be learned from any heartache. Never forget that they taught you how deep your love could be. Never forget the joy you felt around them.

Never forget, because if there's one lesson they taught you, it's that you get high on love if you find the right person. It just wasn't them.

Risking your heart is brave. It's making yourself vulnerable to pain for a chance at experiencing pure bliss somewhere along the way.

It's allowing yourself to love when you know there might be a painful fall. It's loving big in a world that expects you to love small.

Now that is bravery.

Life is too short to be played safely. To not risk your heart out. To not chase your dreams. To not tell the people you love how much they mean to you because you're afraid of scaring them off with your big feelings.

Life is too short to not submit your application because you're afraid you're not good enough. To not give that pretty girl your phone number because your fear is telling you she'll laugh at you or say no.

Do not let the fear of failure take away your shot at happiness.

It's not that I'm not afraid anymore. But now I know I'll get through it—no matter what.

There are still things that terrify me. Tons of them. Some are constant, lingering thoughts in the back of my head. Those thoughts are not rational and they'd rarely make sense to an outsider, but I assure you, they sure feel real, and out of my control too.

Anxiety fills my mind with self-doubt and pure conviction that the one-in-a-billion will happen to me or that it already has.

For the longest time, my anxiety controlled almost every aspect of my life. I didn't live the experiences I wanted most: the satisfaction of chasing my dreams, the buzz from meeting new people, and the pleasure in traveling to a new place. I was too afraid.

I was afraid I'd fail. Screw something up. Say the wrong thing. Find myself in a situation where I didn't know what to do, and feel stupid for being there. I was afraid people wouldn't see past my awkward, goofy self and I was afraid I would drown in my anxiety, far from the comfort of home.

And you know what? All these things happened. I failed professionally more times than I care to admit. I met people who didn't like me, and some who did but still left. And I went on trips that went horribly.

But what my fear didn't tell me, and never will, is that even if those things happen, I'm going to be okay. That whatever happens, I'll get through it and always will. The discomfort is temporary—the experiences I gain are lasting.

What my fear didn't tell me is that just because I failed once at a thing doesn't mean I always will. So I'll keep going after my dreams. I'll keep meeting people and I'll keep traveling, too. I'll keep putting myself out there, exposing myself to what I want even if it scares me because I'm never prouder of myself than when I do exactly that. I'll keep failing, and I'll keep surviving.

You see, it's not that I'm unafraid—I'm still terrified, and quite often too. But I won't let fear stop me from living my life. Grab ahold of yours, even if you're scared. Say, "I got this!" because you absolutely do.

be

uncool

You've got friends all around, yet that one relationship consumes your thoughts.

When the person who helped shape you into who you are disappears suddenly, it hurts. They leave you with the shards of a reality you can't seem to fit back together. But they also leave you with unanswerable questions and self-doubt.

Was the love even real?

Could I have said anything to make them stay?

It's weird, grieving a living person. They're here, yet they're not.

You make excuses for them. You look for reasons to stay, ignoring the repeated red flags.

You've convinced yourself that they will come back.

Your despair stops you from confronting reality.

But deep down, you know that they're already gone.

That it's time to walk away.

Hope is not enough to keep a relationship alive forever.

Sometimes, when you love someone, the best thing you can do is to set them free.

Some people aren't meant to stay. No matter how much they change your life, no matter how much you love them—some people are just temporary.

It took me a while to accept that sometimes even the most beautiful relationships end. Sometimes, we lose people we thought would be by our side forever. I'm learning to accept that their absence doesn't have to ruin my memory of them. I'm learning to appreciate what I gained from knowing them rather than to focus on the void their departure created. I think of temporary people as helpers—angels, some would say. They come into your life when you both need each other. You give them a purpose and in dark moments, they brighten your life.

It's no coincidence we get attached to some more than others. Life keeps us close to those who touch our souls. I'm not religious, but that I believe in. I believe in fate. I believe that life puts people in our path so they'll light up the way—I believe we have to trust the process. Looking back, there's been no one that I became attached to who didn't positively affect my life, at least a little.

Some people just come into your life to flip on the lights using a switch that was always there, hidden under a pile of dust that no one had ventured to use before.

I've met these people. Some left, but their lessons remain. I don't love them less now that they're gone—I do miss them, though. The void that their absences leave is healed by the beauty of their lessons. They helped shape me and they taught me to love myself. They are my forever people. There is beauty in the ephemeral, in these short lived connections. Maybe if they hang on too long, the vividness dulls and their message gets lost in the noise.

The key, then, is to let them go before the light between you dims—releasing them onward into the next person's path, to plant the same seeds of beauty and growth that so changed you.

You have to set them free.

I know how tempting it is to hop into your fortress when life throws a curveball. How tempting it is to pretend you don't care, because if you care, you're giving away the power to hurt you.

But believe me, walls are only a temporary relief and can only keep the storm out for so long. So be the open one. Be the one who isn't afraid to feel, to open up and to cry, and to laugh and to live. Do not become aloof because a few souls have crushed your tender heart.

There are moments in life when things don't go as planned and you're left facing your biggest fears. In those moments, it's hard to see the light. Trying times force you to find that light—a light that lives within, a light that waits patiently for its chance to shine. Trying times shape you amid their chaos. They show you how resilient you are and the strength you hold in the trenches of your heart.

If your deepest fear becomes a reality, remember that you are stronger than you ever thought you could be. After all, you've come this far. You've conquered everything thrown at you 'til now. This is no different. In a week, a month, or a year, you'll look back with pride on the scar this battle left on your soul. It's a reminder that despite the fear, you survived the ache. Diamonds are formed under pressure. Don't you forget it.

We strive to connect with people, yet we tend to hide what makes us us: our emotions. Our pasts have taught us that unfiltered feelings scare people away, so we bottle them up.

We protect ourselves and hide our true depth, convinced that the best way to make others interested in us is to act disinterested.

We force ourselves to become someone we're not, sending mixed signals to be the "cool" one. We play hard to get.

We count the minutes before we answer their messages so as not to seem too excited. We're aloof, even though every inch of us is eager to meaningfully connect.

We're afraid to show our true self in case the other person doesn't reciprocate.

If hiding your heart's truth seems safer than opening up, then maybe that person is not for you. The people who are right for you won't make you doubt if you should open your heart to them. They won't make you feel like your feelings are a burden.

They'll make you feel safe. So next time you hesitate to answer that text message, just don't—text them back.

They're not going to run away because you enthusiastically answered right away instead of an hour later.

The next time you feel yourself hesitating to tell someone how happy they make you feel, don't—say it. Let them know the positive impact they have on you. Don't shy away from expressing yourself for fear of their reaction or lack thereof. Don't protect yourself, be the one who dares.

Feelings aren't always mutual, but that doesn't make them any less real. It doesn't make them any less beautiful. You won't meet the person who makes your soul explode if you don't open up. The best things seldom happen inside your comfort zone.

I hope you find the courage to put yourself out there. I hope you risk your heart out for a chance at experiencing long-lasting connections. And above all, I hope you find the people who make you feel safe enough to tear your walls down. I don't know about you but I'm on this earth to connect with those who spark something in me and I won't apologize for feeling and loving deeply.

It took me a while to realize that we get to decide what makes us happy. You can be the most successful person and still not feel satisfied. You can have it all in the eyes of the world and still not be fulfilled. When you live your life to make others proud rather than yourself, you set yourself up for disappointment. I know this because that's what I used to do—I wanted to make people proud, so I did what they wanted rather than what my heart yearned to do. And somewhere along the way, I lost myself.

I felt guilty for even considering breaking out of the box I was in, the degree I was supposed to get, and the job I was supposed to have. But now I know that there is nothing to feel guilty about—not conforming to what people expect you to be isn't selfish, it's brave. You don't have to fit into a mold to be successful. In fact, the most successful people don't. You don't have to take over the family business if you don't want to. You get to choose what makes you happy. You're allowed to change, you're allowed to take up space, and you're allowed to make your own choices.

It can be difficult to be the person who follows their heart, to be the one who dares to do things differently—it's true. Breaking free of the standards we were programmed to follow isn't easy. You're going to make mistakes, you're going to fall, and you're going to doubt yourself. But what your head won't tell you in the moments of self-doubt is that you are going to be okay. Even at your lowest, you're still growing—you're learning to survive the hurt. Sit with those uncomfortable feelings and love yourself even when you're not meeting your own expectations.

To achieve your wildest dreams, you just need to believe in yourself. It's not about what others think you should do, it's about you, and you only.

There's no easy way to survive the loss of a person you've shared some of your best moments with. Going through life without them by your side after having walked every day together is nothing short of cruel. It's painful.

It's getting the best news of your life before realizing they're not there anymore to hear it.

It's the hole in your day where you no longer hear how proud of you they are.

It's the absence of happy tears coming through the phone from their overwhelming joy for you, with you.

It's learning to celebrate without them—finding happiness buried deep inside what looks like pure loneliness.

It's limping along with a broken leg, searching for something, anything for support.

It's looking back, scrutinizing the things that changed, missing the "before"—missing them.

I don't think you ever forget those who leave the biggest marks on your life. You live with those marks and the voids they leave.

Building walls to protect yourself
does not bring the safety you desire.

Hidden away in your fortress,
nobody sees your hurt.

*You feel it
all alone.*

It's difficult being the girl who feels "too much" in a world where logic trumps feelings. It's a constant battle to either quiet your feelings or scare people away. We all do it, some more than others—we hide our hearts to protect them from shattering.

We feel "I love you," but say "that's great." We stay cool, stay detached.

We feel "I miss you," but text "I'll let you know when I'm free." We pretend not to care.

We feel "I need you," but answer "doin' good." We pretend to be strong.

We think we're being cool by perpetrating the falsehood that deep feelings are wrong. We're part of the problem. We're continuing the cycle of loneliness instead of forging a new path toward connection. We play into the idea of "cool," but all it brings us is coldness.

I admire those who are unapologetically themselves. Those who hand out their hearts with every interaction, without fear there'll eventually be nothing left. I aspire to be like them.

If you're the girl who feels "too much," I want you to know that your vulnerability is a gift. It does not make you weak. Don't let them convince you that you're too soft. It is okay to think with your heart. Admirable, even. Loving deep and being in tune with your emotions isn't a fault. One of the most beautiful things about love is that you make your own rules—it's not possible to do it wrong, as long as you're doing it honestly.

You just need to find someone who's in awe of your strong emotional capacity instead of burdened by it. And to find them, you have to keep putting yourself out there—showing the world the hidden treasures that are raw emotions.

Don't make the mistake of letting those memories be painful reminders of what used to feel so warm.

Those memories are reminders of what your heart is capable of feeling.

Embrace your pain. Own those feelings, and make them motivation.

Even the past can be your hope for the future.

When you're thinking of what you've lost, try instead to connect yourself to those moments of pure happiness, of you and them.

Remember how you felt.

Remember that it's possible to feel this way.

Trust that you will again.

Don't protect your fragile heart
by building up walls because when you do nothing gets
in, yes,
but nothing gets out.
Stay open to the happiness that
life has to offer
for us all.

If you love an overthinker, there are things you need to know.

Their neediness isn't simply neediness—it's fear.

I promise you, no one is more tired by their overactive mind than they are. They live with it every day, and wish they could live life without the dozen hypotheticals invading each moment. But they can't.

It's sometimes difficult to see, but there is beauty in overthinking. Those people who are most afraid to hurt are also those ones who love the most. If you love an overthinker, you should appreciate that.

Be there for them.

Tell them you're not going away.

Reassure them.

They are still learning to trust. They're learning to let go of their fears because the one before you walked away after love got a little hard. They are fighting every day to win the biggest battle, the battle against their own mind.

When you lose the one your heart had chosen, there isn't a word to ease the pain. I wish I had the magic phrase to keep your pain at bay, but the truth is, it may hurt for a while.

I know how present they are inside of you, I know you feel them whether your day is busy or calm, from sunrise to sunset.

You had goals together. Goals you know they'll achieve without you. You will accept that. You will move on. You will be okay with that fact: the world spins on, even through your hurt.

You will understand that this pain of yours is useful. At some point, you will. It may not make sense, not yet, not now—but it might in the morning, and sooner than you think. Let this pain be the fuel that impels you.

Imagine the strength you'll feel when one evening you'll stop and think, *I didn't think of them this morning, not all day until right now, and I feel alright about that, more than alright—I finally feel like me.*

Tears are not markings of weakness, signs you've failed, crumbled, or screwed up. Tears are brave. They are truth. They're a piece of your heart expressing itself to the world.

The best tears are the ones that flow when you're finally understood. The relief. The tears that make you grow, the ones that pick you up off the floor and give you strength to fight when all you see is darkness.

Tears are a sign that you are not afraid to feel what you're feeling, for what you're feeling is what you *need* to be feeling.

Tears are the light you need in your darkest moments. They can clear out the fog that conceals the path ahead.

They'll show you new depth to your feelings in directions you may not have known.

What makes you cry is no accident—it's what moves you. Use your tears as your guide. Find your tears and follow them.

Loss is how
the universe steers you

in the right direction.

Stop refreshing your Instagram feed to check for their *like* on your latest post.

Post for you, not for them.

Be your own validation.

If you cheat on her and think it will only affect your relationship, you're naive.

If you cheat on her, you will break her in ways that tear through every layer of her soul, as deep as the love you had, plus one.

You'll break her trust, of course, but not just with you—she will begin to doubt others too, those who love her most. Those who never betrayed her and never would.

You'll break her self-esteem. Standing in front of the mirror, she'll sob at her reflection, wondering where she wasn't enough.

You'll break her optimism. She, who believed in fairytales and the good in all hearts, won't anymore.

But if you do it anyway, if you do the unfixable, then I will be here to remind her that your actions don't define her.

I will be here to remind her that she is beautiful. She is enough, no matter what pulled you to another.

I will be here to remind her that how you treated her is a reflection of you, not her.

I will be here to remind her that people are worthy of her trust even if, ultimately, you were not.

I will be here to remind her that her Prince Charming does exist and you were just a speed bump on the road there.

I will be here to remind her that she's stronger than she ever thought she was.

I will be here to remind her that from these ashes she will shine, brighter and warmer than ever before.

Everyone cares in their own unique way.

For some, it's a daily text. For others, it's knowing no matter how many months it's been that there will always be someone on the end of the line if you call.

For some, it's keeping each other posted every hour of the day, and for others, it's knowing no matter how long it's been since you've seen them, when you do catch up, you're right back in it in an instant.

For some, it's finding time to see them this week. For others, it's less often, but you always make it count.

You can't judge *if* a friend cares without knowing *how* they care. So if *you* care, don't give up on them before you learn how they care.

Perfectly
imperfect

Do not soothe the ache of missing them.

There are always lessons to uncover behind the pain.

Remember why they came, not only why they left.

Ask yourself "is the ephemeral happiness they brought me worth the pain of this moment?"

If so, consider yourself lucky. Some people spend their lives chasing that high.

They might be gone, but now you know what your heart is capable of feeling.

Let this be your guide.

When hope is a distant memory, when your life's all but run dry—resist.

When you feel like nobody gets it, don't say it again, show them—insist.

When even waking up in the morning is a battle, fight—persist.

The world needs your voice. It needs you.

Blurred endings don't feel much like an end.

There's no goodbye, no period to close the sentence, marking the moment you move on to the next. No closure.

Just more and more distance, day after day, until what was once so much more than a memory is now out of focus.

So be thankful for those terrible goodbyes, because they are your line in the sand, the signal that starts the healing.

The truth is, my first and final thoughts each day are still what they once were, but now, those sweet memories corrode me from within. I fear the day they will finally burn right through.

The truth is, music doesn't sound the same. My favorite songs flood me with melancholy because those lyrics that once were so meaningful are not about us anymore.

The truth is, I can't stir honey into yogurt anymore, not without it tasting like you, not without being transported back in time, buried under the weight of emotions.

The truth is, everything reminds me of that night in the cabin. That night we laughed until our faces hurt before I laid my head on your chest, falling asleep to everything about you.

The truth is, I am struggling.

Fizzy anticipation, now a stubborn ache. And against all I thought possible, I hate the love we had. I am bruised from our happiness—a happiness that is gone.

I can't stop caring, I don't know how to stop loving you. I've tried.

I can't force you to love me how I need to be loved. I know this.

I can't force you to be more than you are or can be right now.

I can't force you to be anybody but who you are right now.

I also know that bitterness is a choice. You don't have to be a mistake I made, a choice that shouldn't have happened.

It's okay for beautiful things to end—painful, but okay.

Love changes but it doesn't make past moments less real.

It doesn't require resentment. And it doesn't mean we'd be better having never known each other.

One thing I'm convinced of is no matter how short-lived, these connections that swell your heart's capacity are worth it.

Even if you're buried in feelings that scream to you the contrary, your heart remembers how it felt, that hope, and how to do it again. It takes root in you forever.

Everybody makes mistakes.

Forgive yourself.

This is just a reminder that no matter how much someone's social media shows they have their life together, you only see what they show, the highlight reel they want you to see.

We all struggle, some of us more than most. So remember to remember that it makes sense your behind-the-scenes doesn't seem to compare.

The hardest thing about being cheated on is not knowing which of the hundred emotions you're feeling is the worst. Feeling so much at once that your heart feels it will explode.

It's wondering if maybe they would have stayed if you'd have just tried a little harder, forgetting the old favorite sweatshirt for that sexy dress.

It's wondering if they would have been faithful if your anxiety hadn't weighed them down.

It's wondering if perhaps their heart would not have settled elsewhere if you'd shown interest in their hobby you know nothing about.

When you've been betrayed by the person your heart had chosen, the hardest thing is the constant self-questioning.

It's the not-knowing. It's having to accept that sometimes things don't make sense. Sometimes, things happen that will break you to pieces.

In those moments, you have to remember that this has nothing to do with you. There is someone out there who will love every piece of you. Someone who'll get lost in your baggy eyes and faded mascara. Someone who will smile at your puffy face in the morning and who will wrap their favorite sweatshirt around you to keep you warm— but really just because they want your smell to infuse it.

There is someone out there who can give you everything you've ever wanted in a relationship. Don't settle for less because it's convenient. You deserve more.

Love is not a science. It's not about how long you've known them or how long you've been together.

It's not the numbers. It's the feelings.

It's how your heart felt the first time you saw them. It's how you felt the first time you woke up next to them, and the other times too. It's the lessons they taught you, lessons that will stay forever, lessons that changed you, lifted you to who you are today.

Love is not how long they stayed, but the imprint they left on your soul.

Everything fades. No feeling is permanent. Yet, months have gone by and I still feel the same.

My heart still jumps out of my chest when I hear our song. I still panic when a stranger looks like you. I still stare at my phone hoping your name is the one popping up. I still fantasize about what we could have been if we'd just tried harder.

And then, I remember the reality—you didn't love me like I loved you. I *had* to walk away. I had to make room for someone who'd be able to love me more than you do. Someone who will love me at my worst, someone who will notice when I dye my hair, someone who will miss me when we're away from each other, someone who will hug me when I'm sad, someone who will see the beauty in my quirks, someone who will love me when I don't love myself—not for a few weeks but for the next decades.

Someone who will still look at me with stars in their eyes after the honeymoon phase is over—someone who knows how to care for my fragile heart. This wasn't you, and though I wish I could, I can't make you love me. This is me moving on.

There are moments in our lives that shape us. Moments that push us to better ourselves—to step out of our comfort zone. A few months ago, I realized that the only thing preventing me from making my dreams a reality was fear. Fear had been dictating my every move, or lack thereof. Fear of failure, fear of rejection, fear of being misunderstood, fear of being judged.

Fear is that little voice inside your mind trying to protect you but limiting you. You don't have to listen to it—in fact, you shouldn't. You should do the things that scare you.

You should tell the people you love that they matter to you, even if you're afraid they'll cringe or run away. You should get on that plane, even if you're scared shitless. And you should also apply for that job you've been dreaming of, even if you're afraid of being told 'no.'

Take risks. You will fail sometimes, there's no denying it, but what your fear isn't telling you is that you will grow from it. You'll be okay, no matter what happens.

Don't be the person who plays it safe, the one who's still wondering "what if," because they never took a chance. Be the one who tries, the one who takes risks. Look fear in the eye and go against its advice, even if every fiber of your being is begging you to stay grounded in your comfort zone.

At the end of the day, it's pretty simple. If you want to experience the things that send shivers down your spine and put sparkles in your eyes, you have to take risks. Believe me, the pain you'll feel if your expectations aren't met is nothing compared to the slow torture from that whisper in your mind of "what if?"

If someone close to you commits suicide, you are going to be left with questions.

With what-ifs pounding in your head.

> *What if I had answered that message sooner.*
> *What if I had shared my struggles more.*
> *What if I shared them too much.*
> *What if I'd hugged them tighter.*
> *Made more time for them…*
> *Learned the warning signs…*
> *What if I wasn't a good enough friend.*

You may even ask Google to help fill in your heart's blanks.

> *Why would someone want to die?*
> *Is dying painful?*
> *Why does depression stop you from getting help?*
> *What did I do wrong?*

For that last one, the answer is almost universally this: Nothing. *You did nothing wrong.*

The truth is, if someone truly wants to end their life, that may be the precise moment they're least likely to pick up the phone to share their intentions. They don't want to be talked out of it.

I hate that truth. I hate it. It just…hurts. It hurts to know that so many suffer in silence—suffering so much that, in one desperate moment, they perceive no other way out than the most final of exits.

If you're feeling down while reading this, I want you to know that you are not alone. I don't know you, but I *do* know there are people who care about you, your feelings, and your life. I care. I don't know you, but I care. You deserve to be heard, to be happy. You deserve to live. No one should have to feel that the only solution is a final and permanent one. And no one should make that choice alone when they're in that desperate state of mind.

It truly sucks how depression is so often seen as negative—as shameful. Maybe we could talk about it as easily as we talk about the weather. "I'm not okay today, I need you," coming out of our mouths as naturally as "It's gonna rain today." And maybe, just maybe, talking about these feelings could be the brief reprieve we need, sustained for another day by that moment of connection. Maybe, then, we wouldn't hide our hearts from the world. Maybe, it would make that crucial inch of difference. Just maybe…

When you share your life on social media, you open the door to critics.

Strangers stroll in to peek at your life—carefully curated but still yours.

You give them a glimpse at some honest feelings—with the sharpest edges rounded off.

You invite them into your home—but only to the living room, and obviously not from the angle that shows how your kitchen counter could be reclassified as a sorting center for the U.S. Postal Service.

You even introduce them to the people you love—but hold on, "Kids, get the nail clippers...those dirt-caked claws aren't getting CPS called on me."

Everyone's got their reasons, but most people like having these portholes into others' lives—if nothing else, it's socially acceptable snooping.

However, some of them won't hesitate to point out that messy kitchen or admonish you about how you're doing parenting wrong. They may "respectfully" disagree with a point in your caption. As decent as that may be, multiply it by ten people, and "respectful" starts to feel like something else.

It's easy to forget the person on the other side of the screen, a person with struggles, just like anyone else—depression, a lost job, PTSD, anxiety, low self-esteem, all of the above, or maybe they're just having a bad day.

When someone is cruel, aggressive, or upsetting to you online, what they say about you often says more about them. Hitting you where it hurts or making sure you know every detail of how they would live your life differently isn't winning the internet. It's mean. It can even be mean when it's not intended to be.

So, as pious or justified as we all may think we are, we have to remember that the person on the other side is just a person, too.

To the mom who struggles to get out of bed but who does it every morning with a smile on her face—I admire your strength and wish I could take some weight off for you.

To the teenager feeling desperate after being bullied— friend, I promise you, as much as it feels like the opposite, your life has not even begun. It gets better. Some of the most interesting and successful people were bullied—true iconoclasts. So don't suffer alone. Find someone who cares and make them part of your life.

To the friend who suffers silently behind their beautiful smile—you might be surprised to discover how sharing your truth won't scare away the people who matter. There are people who will listen to the song of your heart and stay—maybe their song sounds the same. Vulnerability is a gift that brings you closer to the people you love. It lessens your sorrows. The risks, though potentially frightening, are short-lived. The gains are lifelong.

To the man with the pit in his stomach from scrolling through Instagram—don't compare your behind-the-scenes to the curated highlight-reels that primarily exist to pump the poster's ego. Everybody struggles and not everything is as shiny as it seems online. You only see what they show you.

To the woman who keeps it together at work and bursts into tears on the drive home—I've been there, too. You're doing a wonderful job. Lean on someone near or far, and don't be ashamed to let those tears release the pressure of the pain inside. Show the world the cracks underneath.

To everyone struggling one way or another, know that whatever you're feeling, someone else has felt it too. Someone else is feeling it right now. You don't know it because we tend to keep it to ourselves. Thus we continue the cycle of loneliness. I know it's little comfort when your soul hurts so deeply, but I promise you, you are not alone.

Trust me when I tell you there are people out there longing to connect and to help you hold the weight of your worries. These people are all around you; professionals, yes, but also strangers, friends, family, neighbors, and there are good people online, too. Sometimes, all it takes is sending out a single message for the world to remind you—you are not alone.

Walking away from a changing relationship is one of the hardest things you can do.

It's hard because you have to fight against yourself.

You have to fight the part of you that's still stuck in the past. The part of you that can't stop thinking about them—of what it used to be like.

You have to fight the part of you that remembers the daily talks on the phone and struggles to understand why the line is now dead.

You have to fight the ache of missing them, your inside jokes, and your fits of laughter.

You have to fight the part of you that wonders why those precious moments are now a thing of the past.

When you feel them slipping away, you hope and pray it's just a phase—a natural valley between the flowing peaks of a normal relationship. Part of you still trusts that things can be good again. Not today, no, but someday. Maybe, hopefully, who knows?

And a part of you still craves them opening up—finally opening up to discuss what's changed, even what you did wrong, if anything.

But deep down, you know. You hope you don't know, but you think you do. Their distance is a sign of time passing by. People change. Relationships change. Love changes.

It's hard to accept this truth—there's no manual to guide you to the assurance you crave.

It's difficult, accepting that the people who once made you the happiest can evaporate, slowly shrinking right in front of you, imperceptible.

You're left empty, a space that is not quick to fill back up.

Just know you did nothing wrong by trying. It's heart-breaking when things change, but that does not mean it's your fault. This is life. Don't hold too tight to a one-sided structure. Eventually, you'll be completely upside-down.

Sometimes, the bravest thing to do is to let go. You need to make room in your heart for someone who chooses you every day. Someone who makes you a priority, on good days or bad—when it's convenient and when it's not. You need to make room for someone who truly loves you.

Be the one who cares.

Be the one who's vulnerable and proud of it.

Be the one who takes a chance on openness, even while knowing how sharp the pain can be.

Be the one who forgives—the one who understands that our mistakes make us humans.

Be the one who'd rather be wrong and kind than mean and trying to be right.

Be the one who dares to be different, who seeks to know themselves.

Be the one who shows up, the one who gives second chances.

Be the one who lives unapologetically and authentically, without fear of judgement.

Be the one who listens to their heart.

Be the one who doesn't take the little things others do for granted.

Be the one who hears "I need you" behind their friends' "I'm good."

Be the one for those who need you, but above all else, do it for you.

Be the one who works to be the best one they can be—the one who's not defined by others' judgment. Be the one who takes the box they've been put in and kicks down all the walls. Be uncool. Be too cool. Be quiet. Be loud. Be soft, be kind, be brave. Be the one.

Be you.

EILEEN LAMB is the founder of The Autism Cafe and author of *All Across The Spectrum*. Born in France, she now lives in Austin, Texas, with her husband and two sons, Charlie and Jude. On her blog, she shares the ups and downs of raising a severely autistic child while being on the autism spectrum herself. In her free time, Eileen enjoys daydreaming, wine, and road trips.

INSTAGRAM.COM/THEAUTISMCAFE

TWITTER.COM/THEAUTISMCAFE

THOUGHT CATALOG Books

Thought Catalog Books is a publishing imprint of Thought Catalog, a digital magazine for thoughtful storytelling, and is owned and operated by The Thought & Expression Company, an independent media group based in Brooklyn, NY. Founded in 2010, we are committed to helping people become better communicators and listeners to engender a more exciting, attentive, and imaginative world. As a publisher and media platform, we help creatives all over the world realize their artistic vision and share it in print and digital forms with audiences across the globe.

ThoughtCatalog.com | **Thoughtful Storytelling**

ShopCatalog.com | **Shop Books + Curated Products**